Cà d'Zan

A PICTORIAL GUIDE

RONALD R. McCARTY

TheRingling

THE JOHN & MABLE RINGLING MUSEUM OF ART

STATE ART MUSEUM OF FLORIDA | FLORIDA STATE UNIVERSITY

This edition copyright © 2018
The John and Mable Ringling Museum of Art
Text and images copyright © 2018
The John and Mable Ringling Museum of Art

First published in 2018 by
The John and Mable Ringling Museum of Art
5401 Bay Shore Road
Sarasota, Florida 34243, USA
ringling.org

ISBN # 978-0-916758-30-1
Library of Congress Control Number: 2018930948

Third printing, 2023
Printed in the USA by Global Printing & Packaging

Front cover: Ca' d'Zan from the southwest
Inside front cover: Architectural drawing of Ca' d'Zan by Earl Purdy
(for Dwight James Baum), c. 1924
Pg. 2: Approach to Ca' d'Zan from the east
Pg. 3: John Ringling, 1892. Courtesy of New College of Florida
Pgs. 4-5: Windows from the west façade of Ca' d'Zan
Pg. 7: Mable Ringling, 1905. Courtesy of Lara Brightwell
Pg. 8: Aerial view of Ca' d'Zan from the southwest
Pg. 10: Portrait of John and Mable Ringling from the playroom ceiling by Willy Pogany, 1926
Pgs. 126-127: Aerial view of Ca' d'Zan from the west
Inside back cover: Decorative terracotta with sunflower motif
Back cover: Mable Ringling, 1905. Courtesy of Lara Brightwell

The typeface on the front cover and title page is taken
from a plaque on the gatehouse of Ca' d'Zan.

CONTENTS

ACKNOWLEDGMENTS

This beautiful book is the result of a team effort. I would like to extend my thanks to Katie Booth and Libby Bennett for their design, to Heidi Taylor for assembling the images, and to David Berry for managing the project. I am grateful to those who have supported me in this endeavor, including Lara Brightwell, Patricia Ringling Buck, Ruth Burton, Jim Dexheimer, Michael Lancaster, Elizabeth Meibers, Charles Ringling II, and Christopher Schueler and his family. Special thanks are due to Harriet Burns Stieff for providing me with access to her father's records and photographs. Thanks also to photographers Giovanni and Christian Lunardi, with whom I have worked to document Ca' d'Zan over the past fifteen years. This project would not have been possible without the assistance of Deborah Walk, who has served The Ringling as archivist and curator for more than a quarter century.

I would like to take this opportunity to thank those who have supported me and my many projects during my nearly forty years at The Ringling. I am grateful to executive director Steven High, the board of trustees of The John and Mable Ringling Museum of Art Foundation, and The Florida State University. I wish to recognize Joan Behrens, Cynthia Duval, Pam Everhart-Fast, Anthony Janson, Karen Myers, Wendy Outland, Pamela Palmer, Bobbi Parks, Lawrence Ruggerio, Elisabeth Telford, Howard and Janice Tibbals, Karen Turner, John Wetenhall, and Thelma Webb Wright. Thanks to the Bolger Foundation, Jacarlene Foundation, and Sarasota Garden Club for their generous contributions to the maintenance of Ca' d'Zan. Thanks also to those who have worked on the restoration of Ca' d'Zan, including Rick Kimble, Paul Miller, Laurie Ossman, Jennifer Parker, David Piurek, Barbara Ramsay, Michelle Scalera, Specialized Property Services, Linda Stevenson, and Geoffrey Steward and the IFACS team.

I am inspired by the legacy of John and Mable Ringling, and hope their memory continues to be honored for generations to come. I would like to dedicate this book to my partner, R. Michael Glasscock, as well as to Kristie Coburn and Valeria Matula, in recognition of their love and support throughout my life.

Ronald R. McCarty

JOHN AND MABLE RINGLING

John Nicholas Ringling was born in 1866 in the small town of McGregor, Iowa. His parents, August and Marie Salome Ringling, were German immigrants of modest means. When his father's harness-making business began to decline, the family was forced to relocate, ultimately settling in Baraboo, Wisconsin.

John was the second youngest of seven brothers and one sister. In 1882, at the age of sixteen, John partnered with his brothers, Albert, Alfred, Charles, and Otto, to found an entertainment business, consisting of a town hall concert and comedy show. Two years later the brothers joined forces with circus owner Yankee Robinson to form the Yankee Robinson and Ringling Bros. Great Double Show. It featured twenty-two performing animals and other acts for an admission fee of twenty-five cents.

LEFT: John Ringling as a clown, c. 1884.
© Circus World Archives

OPPOSITE: Ringling Bros. Circus poster by the Strobridge Lithographing Company, 1905

The brothers divided up their responsibilities, which evolved as the circus grew. Blessed with a good voice, John initially sang and played the bass violin. He also performed the role of "The Dude" in an act called the Dutch Comedian. He later became the advance man, arranging bookings and signing contracts in towns and cities across the country. The Ringling name became synonymous with wholesome family entertainment.

The transport of the circus shifted from wagon to railroad in 1890. This enabled the Ringlings to reach new markets and expand their business. In time they came to rival the renowned Barnum & Bailey Circus, which they acquired in 1907 for $410,000.

With this purchase the Ringlings established themselves as the undisputed "Kings of the Show World." The brothers became very wealthy and built magnificent homes that reflected their great success. John set up residence in Chicago, where he enjoyed the life of an eligible bachelor, known for his impeccable taste and style. This life changed dramatically when he was introduced to the beautiful and charming Armilda Burton.

ABOVE LEFT:
Mable Ringling, c. 1891.
Courtesy of Ruth Burton

ABOVE RIGHT:
The Burton family, 1892.
Courtesy of the Schueler
family

Armilda was born in 1875 in the farming community of Moons, Ohio. She was raised by loving parents, George and Mary Elizabeth Burton, together with four sisters and one brother. Intelligent, attractive, and ambitious, Armilda left home with a sister at the age of sixteen in search of new opportunities.

Various accounts tell of how John and Armilda met, all of which are undocumented. Whatever the details, John began to court Armilda and shower her with expensive gifts. His heart was captured by her grace and charm, and the two were married in Hoboken, New Jersey, in 1905, at which time Armilda changed her name to Mable.

RIGHT: Mable Ringling, 1905.
Courtesy of Lara Brightwell

LEFT: John and Mable
Ringling at the circus
in Chicago, c. 1919

In 1910 the couple moved into a new luxury apartment building on Fifth Avenue in New York City (later demolished to make way for Rockefeller Center). Occupying the entire sixth floor, their enormous apartment had high ceilings and marble fireplaces in the main living areas. Mable decorated with fine furnishings and crystal chandeliers, paid for by John with profits from the circus and other businesses.

The following year the Ringlings purchased twenty acres of waterfront property in Sarasota, Florida. Acquired from Ralph and Ellen Caples, the property formed part of the exclusive Shell Beach subdivision, previously owned by circus manager and land developer Charles

Thompson. The property included an existing wood-frame house, named Palms Elysian, which the Ringlings used as a winter residence and family vacation destination. It featured twelve rooms and extensive verandas overlooking a semi-tropical landscape.

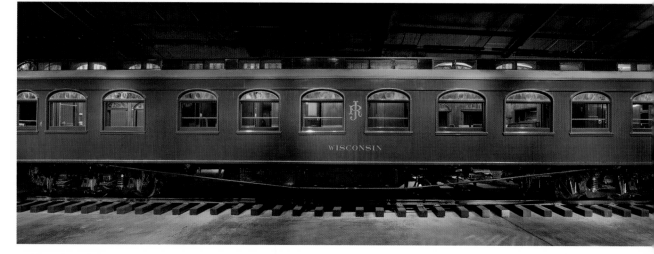

ABOVE:
Wisconsin dining room

RIGHT: *Wisconsin*

OPPOSITE: (Top to bottom)
John and Mable Ringling
with a young guest on
the *Zalophus*, 1920s.
Courtesy of Lara
Brightwell

Ship's wheel from the
Zalophus. Gift of the
Dixon family

Zalophus, 1920s

TRAVELING IN STYLE

John and Mable spent much of their time traveling for business and pleasure. In 1905 they acquired a private Pullman railcar named the *Wisconsin* after the home state of the Ringling Bros. Circus. The railcar was nearly eighty feet long and weighed some sixty-five tons. It was lavishly decorated to Mable's specifications, reflecting her elegant taste and style. It was later replaced by a second, larger railcar, the name of which – the *Jomar* – was a combination of the names John and Mable Ringling.

In addition to railcars, the Ringlings owned a number of yachts, which became increasingly large as their fortune grew. The most impressive of these, the *Zalophus*, was commissioned by John in 1922 for $200,000. The 125-foot yacht was designed by Henry Gielow and manufactured by the Consolidated Shipbuilding Corporation in New York City. Manned by a crew of twelve, the yacht featured six elegant staterooms. It was often used to tour prospective investors around John's real estate developments on the barrier islands of Sarasota. Unfortunately, the yacht sank in 1930 a mile off Lido Beach.

The Ringlings' numerous automobiles also reflected their wealth and status. John's favorite car was the *Czarina*, a 1914 Silver Ghost Rolls Royce originally built for the Czar of Russia. Mable favored a 1923 Pierce Arrow sedan, which she loved to drive herself. The automobiles were parked in a separate garage later incorporated into the original Circus Museum.

The Ringlings took annual trips to Europe, where John searched for new circus acts. It was on these trips that he and Mable developed their love of art and architecture. They traveled in great comfort and style, always as first class passengers, on some of the most famous ocean liners of the day, including the *Aquitania*, *Bremen*, *Leviathan*, and *Mauretania*.

CA' D'ZAN

PREVIOUS PAGE:
East façade of Ca' d'Zan tower

ABOVE: Ca' d'Zan terrace
under construction, c. 1924

RIGHT: Ca' d'Zan tower
under construction, c. 1925

OPPOSITE: Ca' d'Zan, 1927.
© Bettmann/CORBIS

In 1924 the Ringlings hired New York architect Dwight James Baum to design a house to replace Palms Elysian, to better reflect their wealth and social status. Completed two years later, at a cost of $1.5 million, the new mansion stands more than eighty feet high by 200 feet wide, and occupies 36,000 square feet. It is the largest and most spectacular private residence built on the west coast of Florida during the real estate boom of the 1920s.

While the mansion is named Ca' d'Zan, meaning "House of John" in Venetian dialect, it more accurately reflects the tastes of Mable, who was directly involved in all aspects of its development. Baum designed the mansion in the style of a Venetian Gothic palace, like those admired by Mable on her trips to Italy. The mansion incorporates elements from Mable's favorite Venetian palazzos, such as Ca' d'Oro on the Grand Canal and the Doge's Palace at St. Mark's Square. Mable kept drawings and photographs of these historic buildings, which she shared with Baum, who also accompanied her to Venice on several occasions.

LEFT: Owen Burns (left) and Dwight James Baum, 1925. Courtesy of the Burns family

OPPOSITE TOP: Postcard of the Sarasota County Courthouse, 1950s. © State Archives of Florida, Florida Memory

OPPOSITE BOTTOM: El Vernona Hotel, 1925. Courtesy of the Burns family

ARCHITECTS AND BUILDERS

Architect Dwight James Baum was a specialist in residential design, who produced work in various revival styles then popular in America. In 1923 he became the youngest ever recipient of the prestigious Gold Medal of the Architectural League of New York, an accomplishment that greatly impressed the Ringlings.

Baum's main office was in Riverdale-on-Hudson, New York. During his work on Ca' d'Zan, he set up a branch office in Sarasota, where he carried out a number of other significant projects, including the Sarasota County Courthouse. He was assisted at Ca' d'Zan by on-site architects Earl Purdy and Ralph Twitchell. Later, Twitchell established his own office in Sarasota and became a founding member of the Sarasota School of Architecture.

Construction of Ca' d'Zan was overseen by general contractor Owen Burns, with help from engineer Lyman Dixon. Burns was a major local landowner who did much to develop Sarasota in the early twentieth century. He built the El Vernona Hotel (later renamed the John Ringling Hotel), designed by Baum, and the causeway linking Sarasota to the barrier islands, paid for by John Ringling.

Mable was actively involved in the construction of Ca' d'Zan, working with Burns to make numerous changes to the building as the project advanced. While this created tension with Baum during his visits to the site, John resolved all disputes, ensuring that Mable's requests were carried out exactly as specified.

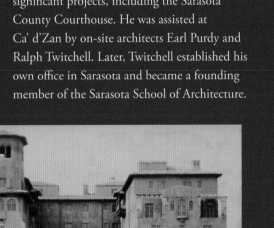

The mansion features fifty-six rooms. Those used by the Ringlings and their guests are situated on three sides of a central court. To the south are service areas, including a pantry, kitchen, laundry room, and sleeping quarters for the staff. Above the main three-story building is an additional two-story tower, inspired by the tower of the old Madison Square Garden in New York City, where John had an office. The tower at Ca' d'Zan consists of a guest bedroom below and open belvedere above. Accessed via an external staircase, the belvedere offers panoramic views of Sarasota Bay and Longboat Key.

The exterior of the mansion is covered in rose-colored stucco and clad in glazed and unglazed terracotta, much of which features representations of flora and fauna, reflecting Mable's love of nature. Mable traveled with Baum to the factory of the O. W. Ketchum Terra Cotta Works in Crum Lynne, Pennsylvania, where she inspected the kilns (by climbing into them) and selected the final colors and glazes.

The roof of the mansion consists of thousands of multi-colored ceramic tiles from demolished buildings in Granada, Spain. The steps of the main entrance are paved in rare Formosa marble from Germany. The waterside terrace and lower dock are paved in five different marbles from Europe and America, laid out in a chevron pattern. Approached from the court via seven doors of multi-colored, English lac glass, the terrace was used by the Ringlings to entertain as many as 500 guests.

After its completion, Ca' d'Zan was documented in a number of national publications. A full-page illustration of the west elevation was featured in an issue of *The American Architect* in 1926. An exclusive article on the mansion, describing its design and decoration, was printed in *Country Life* the following year.

OPPOSITE: West façade of Ca' d'Zan

BELOW: *Country Life* magazine, 1927

BOTTOM: Gray Crag, 1935.
© Palisades Interstate Park Commission

GRAY CRAG

During the summer months, when the heat and humidity in Sarasota were excessive, the Ringlings spent much of their time at an estate in Alpine, New Jersey, overlooking the Hudson River. Purchased by the Ringlings in 1919, the estate, named Gray Crag, consisted of 100 acres of property with a large residence, separate guesthouses, and other service buildings. Mable oversaw the landscaping of the property, which included formal gardens on a street known appropriately as Millionaire's Row.

DECORATORS AND CRAFTSMEN

Mable oversaw the interior decoration of Ca' d'Zan, focusing specifically on painted finishes and marble installations. Much of the finishing work was carried out by European craftsmen supervised by principal decorator Robert Webb, Jr., who had been a student of painter John Singer Sargent. Webb contributed to the decoration of other local properties designed by Baum, including the El Vernona Hotel and the Sarasota County Courthouse.

ABOVE: Robert Webb's signature

FAR LEFT: Closet door

LEFT: Robert Webb, 1950s. Courtesy of Thelma Webb Wright

The ceilings of the ballroom and playroom at Ca' d'Zan were painted by Hungarian artist William (Willy) Andrew Pogany, a well-known book illustrator and set designer for ballets, operas, and films. Pogany was introduced to the Ringlings by their close friend, Florenz Ziegfeld, owner of the famous Ziegfeld Follies, who stayed at Ca' d'Zan with his wife, the actress Billie Burke (who played the role of Glinda the Good Witch in the film, *The Wizard of Oz*). Pogany later moved to California where he worked for newspaper magnate William Randolph Hearst, whose grand residence, Hearst Castle, in San Simeon, is contemporary with Ca' d'Zan.

WILLY POGANY

ABOVE LEFT: Self-portrait of Willy Pogany from the playroom ceiling, 1926

LEFT: Willy Pogany's signature

ABOVE: Detail of the ballroom ceiling

PRINCIPAL ROOMS

FOYER

The front door of Ca' d'Zan leads into the foyer, or entrance hall. Originally intended by Baum as the living room, the foyer was spacious enough to be used by Mable for luncheons and other gatherings. The view of the court, directly to the west, is framed with arches supported by columns clad with rare Mexican onyx, acquired by the Ringlings during a trip to California. In front of the columns are gilt throne chairs purchased from the estate of railroad owner George Jay Gould. Flanking the front door, faced in polished mahogany, are a pair of seventeenth-century Flemish tapestries. These hang above two antique Italian cassoni, or wedding chests, which once stored paper music rolls for the Aeolian organ located nearby.

On the south wall, near the entrance to the dining room, is a portrait of *Mariana of Austria, Queen of Spain*, produced by the workshop of Diego Velázquez in c. 1656. Below the portrait stands a French commode, which is a fine reproduction of an original made in 1739 for Louis XV, King of France, for his private chambers at Versailles. While the original housed the king's collection of presentation medals, the reproduction stored Mable's monogrammed bridge cards, score tablets, and phonograph records.

ABOVE: *Mariana of Austria, Queen of Spain* by the workshop of Diego Velázquez, c. 1656

LEFT: French commode

SOLARIUM

Located at the northeast corner of the mansion, the solarium was originally used as an entertainment pavilion for garden parties and poolside events. The three exterior walls are lined with arched windows and doors framed in terracotta. The lower portion of the framework features a Gothic pinwheel design, copied from one of Mable's favorite Venetian buildings, the Palazzo Contarini Fasan. A winged lion, the symbol of Venice, appears in each corner of the decorative ceiling, painted by Robert Webb. The floor is covered in a geometric pattern of green and purple marble.

BELOW:
Detail of winged lions
from the solarium ceiling

OPPOSITE:
Solarium facing west

RECEPTION ROOM

While it functioned primarily as a reception and sitting area, this room could also be cleared of furniture to serve as an extension to the ballroom immediately to the west, with which it shares an Asian teak floor, perfect for dancing. As was originally the case, when not in use as a single space, the two rooms are separated with a three-panel screen by the French interior design firm of Jules Allard et Fils.

The south side of the reception room, nearest the foyer, features two twisted (Solomonic) columns, of carved and gilded wood, purchased by the Ringlings in Venice. Opposite the columns is an equally impressive carved and gilded doorway, also from Italy, providing access to the solarium.

The reception room displays many of the Ringlings' most prized possessions, collected over twenty-five years of marriage. In the center of the room is a French bureau-plat, or writing desk, at which Mable drafted her correspondence. Atop the desk are a silver vase and bronze humidor, both by Tiffany & Company. The vase was used by Mable to display roses from her garden, while the humidor was filled with John's favorite Lincoln & Ulmer O-Nic-O cigars. Beneath the desk is a Napoleon III Aubusson carpet that continues the theme of flora and fauna carried throughout the house.

OPPOSITE: View of the reception room from the foyer

RIGHT: Doorway from the reception room to the solarium

BALLROOM

Perhaps the most dramatic room in Ca' d'Zan is the ballroom, used by the Ringlings to entertain family and friends. The room features an elaborate coffered ceiling, covered in shiny gold leaf. The ceiling incorporates twenty-two vignettes painted by Willy Pogany in 1926. Titled *Dancers of the Nations*, they depict dancing couples in native costumes from around the world. Four additional vignettes in the corners illustrate dances popular throughout American history. These culminate in the tango, the dance craze of the Ringlings' day.

Around the room is a set of carved and gilded chairs and couches, which provided seating during the many musicals held at the mansion. The set is a nineteenth-century reproduction of a celebrated suite of English furniture made around 1700 for the first Duke of Leeds. Also of note are an Asian gong, used to announce the start of musical performances, and a group of three antique Venetian mirrors that reflected the light during evening gatherings.

OPPOSITE: Ballroom facing west

BELOW: View of the ballroom facing east toward the reception room

FOLLOWING PAGES: Ballroom ceiling

COURT

Originally designed as a courtyard open to the sky, the court was ultimately enclosed, on Baum's recommendation, to protect it from the elements. This large living room was the center of activity at Ca' d'Zan, where it was used by the Ringlings primarily for the purpose of entertaining. Surrounded on three sides by a balcony, supporting a mezzanine above, the room rises at the center to more than thirty feet in height. The coffered ceiling of pecky cypress features Venetian-inspired decorative motifs painted by Robert Webb. A skylight of multi-colored, English lac glass provides the space with the natural light that Mable desired.

The black and white marble floor is symbolic of the Masonic order, of which John was a member. Hanging above is a crystal chandelier from the old Waldorf Astoria Hotel in New York City, which was torn down in 1929 to make room for the Empire State Building. A Renaissance-style fireplace on the north wall was used to warm guests on cool winter evenings. The current layout of the furniture, in small groups enabling intimate conversation, is based on photographs of Mable's original arrangement.

OPPOSITE:
Court facing north

BELOW: Court, 1920s

FOLLOWING PAGES:
Court ceiling and skylight

Along the south wall is the Aeolian organ, acquired by the Ringlings in 1924 for $25,000. The mansion was built around this impressive instrument, the 2,289 pipes of which are housed in a chamber on the second and third floors. It is said that when the doors to the terrace were open, the sound from the pipes could be heard across the bay.

In the northwest corner of the court is a Steinway grand piano with a beautiful rosewood case, dating from 1892. Here John's nephew and niece, Robert and Hester Ringling, gave musical recitals. Robert became a singer with the Civic Opera in Chicago.

RIGHT: View of the court with the Aeolian organ

OPPOSITE TOP: Portraits of John and Mable Ringling by Savely Sorine, 1927

OPPOSITE BOTTOM: Postcard of the court, 1950s

RINGLING PORTRAITS

On the south wall of the court hang watercolor portraits of John and Mable, dating from 1927. They are the work of popular Russian portraitist Savely Sorine, whose sitters included Princess Elisabeth, the future Queen of England. Sorine was introduced to the Ringlings in New York City, where he had opened a studio earlier in the decade.

The Ringlings were painted in the solarium, chosen for the quality of the light from the windows. In the finished portraits, John is shown standing in a Florida landscape, suggestive of his interests in local real estate, while Mable is depicted sitting in an opera box, reflective of her love of the arts.

BREAKFAST ROOM

South of the court is the subtle but elegant breakfast room, used for informal dining. The room is decorated in Mable's favorite color, green. The color features in the glass of the chandelier, made in Murano, Italy, and on the custom-painted Renaissance-style chairs. Green is also the color of the Venetian blinds in the windows, which can be opened to reveal views of the bay.

While the Ringlings had no children, they did have a family of pets, including a German shepherd, miniature pinschers, and a variety of exotic birds. The wrought-iron gates in the entryway, leading into the breakfast room from the court, were likely installed to keep the dogs out during meals. Mable placed bird-stands in the room for her scarlet macaws, which matched a bird depicted in one of her favorite paintings, *Still Life with Parrots*, produced by Flemish artist Jan Davidsz de Heem in the late 1640s. Hung for many years on the north wall of the breakfast room, the painting is now displayed in the art museum.

OPPOSITE: Breakfast room facing south

LEFT: *Still Life with Parrots* by Jan Davidsz de Heem, late 1640s

TAPROOM

The taproom was acquired by John in 1925 from the Cicardi Restaurant in St. Louis, Missouri. It is perhaps the most surprising feature of a house built during the Prohibition era.

The room is paneled in rich black walnut and decorative stained glass. The doors behind the Art Deco bar conceal a refrigerator and pair of sinks, used in the preparation of cocktails. The alcohol served here was stored in a vault on the third floor, hidden behind a false wall.

The colorful floor of the taproom comprises pieces of marble broken during the installation of the waterside terrace. High above, on the south wall, hangs an impressive pair of longhorns given to John by his friend and fellow art collector, Amon Carter, of Fort Worth, Texas.

BELOW: Taproom facing northwest

OPPOSITE: Taproom facing southeast

DINING ROOM

The formal dining room is without question the most opulent room in the mansion. The walls are covered in rich black walnut, with neoclassical details, removed from a Gilded Age mansion in New York City. The French marble fireplace along the south wall was used to warm the room on cool winter evenings. Centered above the mantle hangs a decorative tondo from the Della Robbia workshop in Florence, Italy.

The most striking feature of the room is the decorative ceiling, featuring an Islamic star pattern. While it gives the appearance of hand-carved wood, the ceiling is actually molded plaster painted by Robert Webb. The design includes elements inspired by Mable's collection of antique cameos and intaglios, lent to Webb for the purpose.

The monumental dining table was made in Paris by the firm of Jules Allard et Fils. The table includes twenty leaves that can expand its length to thirty feet. In the Ringlings' day, the table was rolled into the foyer or court for large events. The Renaissance-style dining chairs are upholstered in rich ruby-red velvet. The table setting includes a Venetian lace tablecloth and a pair of Bohemian covered cups of exceptional size and quality.

On the west wall hangs a pair of Palladian-style mirrors of carved and gilded wood, made by John and Frances Booker in Dublin, Ireland, around 1755. Suspended above is a silver-plated chandelier by Edward F. Caldwell & Company, a New York lighting firm that produced elegant fixtures for a number of other notable residences, including the White House and Biltmore, the Vanderbilt estate in Asheville, North Carolina.

OPPOSITE:
Dining room facing southeast

BELOW: Dining room, 1940s

FOLLOWING PAGES:
Dining room ceiling and chandelier

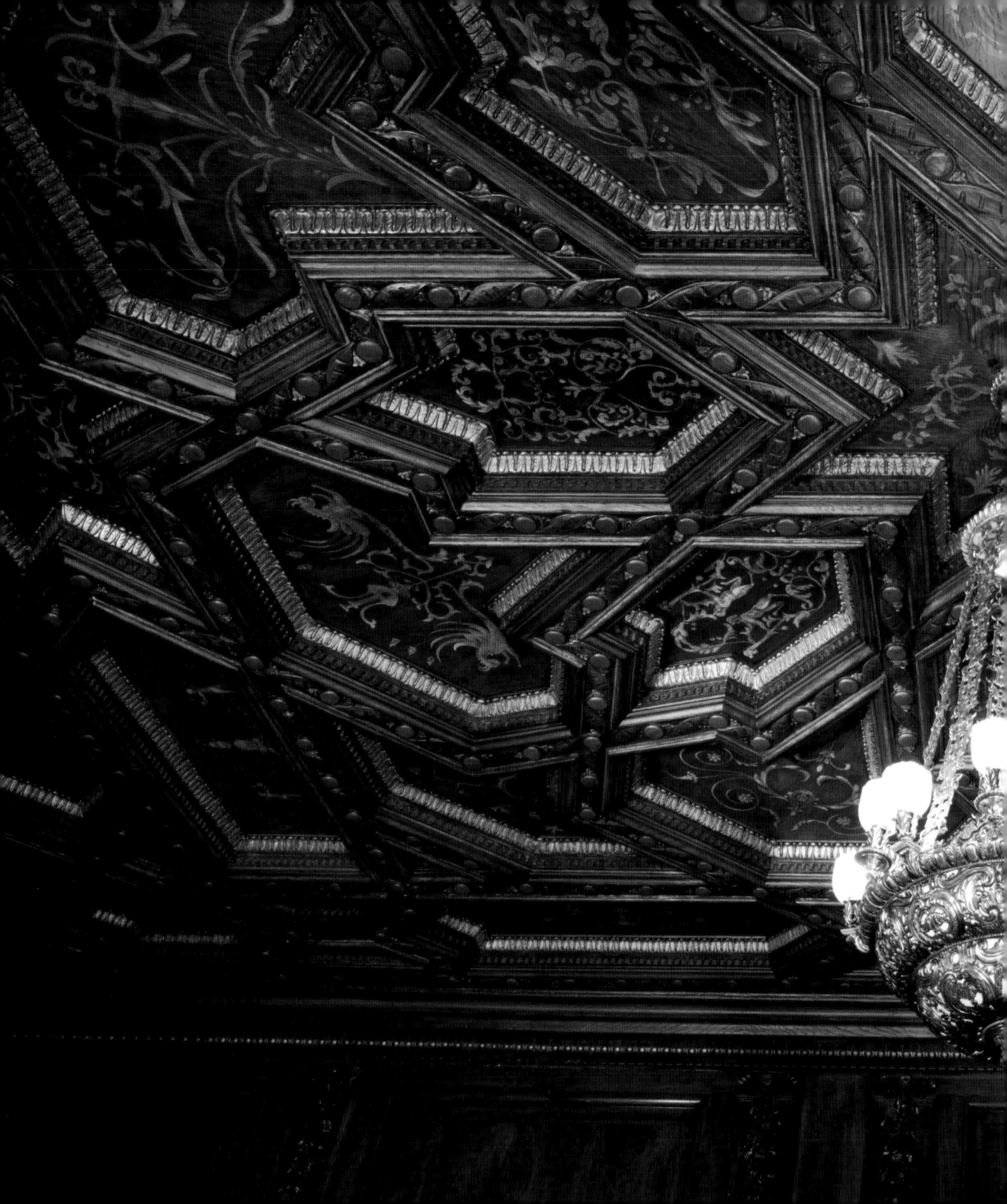

PANTRY

The pantry was one of the most active service areas of Ca' d'Zan. In the center of the room, two large wooden tables were originally used to prepare the meals served to guests in the breakfast and dining rooms.

The pantry is equipped with a warming oven and set of refrigerators, which still have the original ice trays. The most notable feature of the room is a custom-made, German silver sink stretching the entire length of the north wall. The sink's soft metal surface (made of an alloy of copper, nickel, and zinc) was intended to protect from breakage the Ringlings' fine china and earthenware, displayed in glass-front cabinets located nearby.

A small butler's pantry, directly to the west, contains a selection of silverware used at formal gatherings held at the mansion. In the Ringlings' day, the room was also used to store Mable's table linens, which featured her embroidered monogram.

TABLEWARE

The Ringlings owned an extensive collection of crystal, silverware, china, and earthenware acquired during the course of their travels. The collection includes formal services and casual sets by such notable makers as Tiffany, Wedgwood, Quimper, and Cantagalli. The variety of tableware enabled the Ringlings to cater for any occasion.

OPPOSITE:
Napkin monogramed with the initials of Mable Ringling

TOP: Duck-shaped decanter set

ABOVE:
Selection of fine silver

LEFT: Tiffany flatware and table setting from Imola, Italy

ABOVE: Westinghouse range
(left) and Vulcan stove

OPPOSITE:
Kitchen facing northeast

KITCHEN

The large and spacious kitchen was appointed with the most up-to-date equipment available at the time. Meals were cooked on a cast-iron, Vulcan gas stove and a custom-made, Westinghouse electric range. Wooden doors in the north wall conceal electric Kelvinator refrigerators, large enough for hanging meats.

The walls of the kitchen are painted Mable's favorite color, green. The color gave the room a sense of calm even when it was bustling with activity. The original paint contained trace amounts of arsenic, added for the purpose of pest control. The east and west walls include large windows, providing the room with natural light.

RIGHT: Mable Ringling's maid, Hedwig Thomlinson, 1920s. Courtesy of the Heusted family

BELOW: Annunciator panel

OPPOSITE: View of the staircase and elevator lobby from the foyer

STAFF QUARTERS

Ca' d'Zan was run by a staff of eight, consisting of a butler and seven servants. These included a Swedish chauffeur and German cook, who presided over the kitchen and pantry. The staff was kept very busy, catering to the every need of the Ringlings and their guests.

South of the kitchen is a room originally used for dining by the staff. The room features a communication device called an annunciator, which enabled guests to request assistance by pressing a button in their rooms. The button would ring a bell on the annunciator panel, informing the staff that help was required.

A spiral staircase leads up to rooms on the second floor used as sleeping quarters by the staff during the Ringlings' day. The rooms were simply furnished and all include windows, offering views of the grounds and bay.

STAIRCASE AND ELEVATOR LOBBY

Providing access to the upper floors of the mansion is a grand staircase that begins in an elevator lobby to the south of the foyer. The gracefully curving staircase features white marble wainscoting, cut in a scallop pattern, as well as a yellow marble handrail and border. The walls of the staircase and lobby are covered in textured stucco, painted to give a marble-like appearance.

Ca' d'Zan was one of the first private residences in Florida to contain an elevator, which provided guests with easy access to all floors. The Ringlings purchased the elevator from the Otis Elevator Company in 1926 for $5,000. The elevator door at lobby level is framed with a decorative border of cast stone, matching framework in the vestibule on the second floor.

JOHN RINGLING'S MASTER SUITE

The largest and most impressive room on the second floor is John's master suite. The walls of the room are painted a deep blue-green color, while the moldings around the doors and windows are gilded in 23-carat gold leaf. The floor is bordered in rich black marble with golden veins, imported from Italy.

Doors open out from the room onto three balconies, the largest of which, facing east, was shared with Mable, whose suite is next door. The doors and windows flood John's room with natural light and offer views of the grounds and bay.

The room is furnished with a gilt-bronze and mahogany bedroom suite made by Maison Krieger, a premier furniture maker based in Paris. Acquired by John at auction for $35,000, the thirteen-piece suite, including a pair of beds, was decorated with classical motifs.

OPPOSITE:
John Ringling's master suite facing southwest

BELOW: John Ringling's master suite, 1940s

Above a large chest of drawers along the north wall hangs a portrait of *Pauline Bonaparte Borghese* painted in 1811 by French artist Louis Benjamin Marie Devouge. One of John's earliest art purchases, this portrait of Napoleon's sister was acquired around 1916 from the St. Nicholas Hotel in Cincinnati, Ohio.

The ceiling of the bedroom features a painting of *Dawn Driving Away the Darkness* by Dutch artist Jacob de Wit, dating from 1735. At John's request, Robert Webb added cloudscapes to the four corners of the ceiling, which were removed during renovations (under Webb's supervision) in the 1960s.

OPPOSITE: North wall with chest of drawers and portrait of *Pauline Bonaparte Borghese*

ABOVE: *Dawn Driving Away the Darkness* by Jacob de Wit, 1735

FASHION

John was widely regarded as one of the best-dressed men of his day. His wardrobe consisted of clothing and accessories custom-made by the finest designers in Europe and America. Of particular note are his colorful silk neckties, produced by Charvet of Paris.

OPPOSITE: John Ringling's clothing and furniture from his bedroom suite

TOP: John Ringling, 1927

ABOVE: John Ringling's clothing and accessories

JOHN RINGLING'S BATHROOM

John's bathroom is located directly to the southeast of his master suite. The walls of the bathroom are covered in large sheets of yellow marble, which match a six-foot bathtub carved from a single block of stone. The floor is paved in yellow and black marble in a checkered pattern. Robert Webb painted a faux-marble finish on the porcelain commode in keeping with the rest of the room.

The gilt-bronze legs of the sink support a marble vanity with fixtures matching those of the bathtub. The tall mahogany shaving stand, with revolving mirror and magnifier, was perfect for John, who stood six feet four inches in height.

OPPOSITE:
View of John Ringling's bathroom from his master suite

BELOW:
Shaving stand

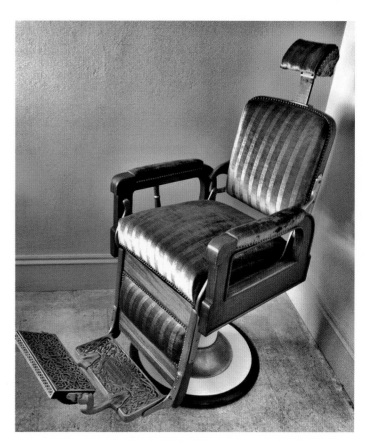

JOHN RINGLING'S OFFICE

Located immediately to the northwest of John's master suite is a small office used for business. Resting on the handsome desk, made by Hobbs & Company of London, is a silver-plated telephone decorated with a floral motif.

Attached to the office is an exercise room, which John used to recuperate after a stroke in 1932. The room features a stand-up shower, barber chair, massage table, and reduction machine, designed to shed inches off the waist and relieve back pain.

OPPOSITE:
John Ringling's office facing west

ABOVE:
Barber chair

MABLE RINGLING'S MASTER SUITE

John and Mable had separate but adjoining bedrooms, as was customary at the time. Located on the east side of the mansion, Mable's master suite offers views of her beloved gardens. French doors open out onto a small balcony fitted with flower boxes, where Mable planted blooming vines that cascaded over the side.

The walls of the room are covered in a fine linen fabric, painted by Robert Webb in a pinstripe pattern of soft earth tones. Webb also decorated the beamed ceiling with heraldic shields and punctuation marks, the meaning of which remains a mystery.

The room is furnished with a stunning bedroom suite, made in Paris in the early 1900s by the famous French ébéniste François Linke. Designed in the Louis-XV style, the suite features marquetry panels depicting floral bouquets, and gilt-bronze mounts, including a playful monkey on a swing.

On the mirrored dressing table stand three statuettes of female figures, two of cast bronze and one of ivory. These are the work of German artist Johann Philipp Ferdinand Preiss, one of the most prolific sculptors of the Art Deco period.

OPPOSITE: Mable Ringling's master suite facing southeast with a view of John Ringling's master suite and bathroom beyond

RIGHT: Female figure by Johann Philipp Ferdinand Preiss, 1900s

OPPOSITE: Mable
Ringling's bedspread

THIS PAGE: Selection
of upholstery fabrics

TEXTILES

Mable had a love of textiles, which she
incorporated throughout Ca' d'Zan. In
addition to sumptuous upholstery fabrics,
such as velvet, she collected fine linens and
lace. A prime example is her bedspread,
consisting of seventeen different pieces of
lace acquired over the years.

MABLE RINGLING'S BATHROOM

To the north of Mable's master suite is her bath and dressing room. Robert Webb enlivened the room with depictions of flowers. The purple and yellow marble of the floor wraps around the white porcelain bathtub, set in an arched alcove at the back of the room. Four mirrored closet doors along the north wall originally concealed Mable's formal attire, while a fifth glass door once displayed her favorite hats and other accessories.

RIGHT:
Mable Ringling's dress. Gift of the Schueler family

OPPOSITE:
View of Mable Ringling's bathroom from her master suite

GUEST BEDROOMS

A door from Mable's bathroom leads to the first of five guest bedrooms on the second floor, used by visiting family. The first room, nearest to Mable's master suite, was reserved for her mother and sisters, with whom she was very close.

The color scheme for each of the five rooms was based on one of the colors of glass—purple, pink, gold, green, and blue—of the windows throughout Ca' d'Zan. The rooms were decorated with fine furnishings and antiques, selected with comfort and luxury in mind. The beds were all fitted with silk crepe sheets bearing Mable's monogram.

While all the rooms have windows, providing natural light, two have balconies, overlooking the grounds and bay. The floors are variously covered in carpet, wood, and Spanish tiles painted with pomegranates and sunflowers.

OPPOSITE: Guest bed

RIGHT: Guest bedrooms

The guest bathrooms all feature glazed floor and wall tiles, in bold colors, as well as marble sinks with glass legs. Mable requested Robert Webb to paint the insides of the medicine cabinet doors with Asian-inspired subjects, intended to surprise and delight her guests.

OPPOSITE: Medicine cabinet doors

ABOVE: Guest bathrooms

MEZZANINE

The guestrooms are all accessed via a hallway that runs along the three sides of the mezzanine, open to the court below. The doors to the guestrooms, facing the hallway, are embellished with Arcadian landscapes attributed to Keppa Buck, the brother of animal collector and adventurer Frank Buck, who once toured with the Ringling Bros. and Barnum & Bailey Circus.

The mezzanine offers views of the Ringlings' collection of seventeenth-century Flemish tapestries, which hang above all four sides of the court. One of the finest is *The Defeated Pompey Fleeing from Caesar*, woven by Guillaume van Leefdael and Geraert van der Strecken, which John purchased at the Vincent Astor Sale in New York City in 1926. The tapestry hangs on the south wall, where it conceals the pipes (and baffles the sound) of the organ below.

The balustrade and columns of the mezzanine are made of rose-colored terracotta. The columns support a decorative frieze, of glazed terracotta, situated directly below the pecky cypress ceiling. In the four corners of the hallway hang lights made from gondoliers' lamps acquired in Venice.

BELOW: *The Defeated Pompey Fleeing from Caesar* by Guillaume van Leefdael and Geraert van der Strecken, 1600s

OPPOSITE: View of the court from the mezzanine

PLAYROOM

The large playroom occupies more than 2,000 square feet of the third floor. It was used to entertain gentlemen guests, who enjoyed smoking, drinking, and playing cards.

The floor of the room is paved in reddish-orange terracotta tiles, purchased by the Ringlings in Cuba. Directly above is a vaulted canvas ceiling, painted with whimsical scenes of Carnival in Venice by Willy Pogany, who depicted himself near the entrance with bucket and brush in hand. The most prominent scene features John serenading Mable, both dressed in festive costumes and surrounded by their various pets. The Ringlings posed for Pogany at his studio in New York City, where the canvas was painted prior to installation.

OPPOSITE: Playroom facing north

BELOW: Hippocampus ornaments from Mable Ringling's gondola

FOLLOWING PAGES: Playroom ceiling

ABOVE: Wine rack

RIGHT: John Ringling's bourbon and other bottles

OPPOSITE: Vault door

Hidden behind a false wall on the east side of the hallway, leading to the playroom from the staircase, is a large walk-in vault, used by the Ringlings to store their most prized possessions when they were not in residence. The vault is fitted with a rack, capable of storing hundreds of bottles of wine and spirits, including John's own reserve stock of bourbon.

TOWER

The tower features a guest bedroom and open belvedere, occupying the fourth and fifth floors of the mansion respectively. The bedroom was used by the Ringlings' most distinguished visitors, including politicians and celebrities of the day. The room is furnished with an antique Italian bedstead and painted Venetian vanity and commode. The floor is bordered with painted Spanish tiles, while the ceiling is covered with mahogany panels and beams with carved acanthus-leaf corbels. The windows, facing all four directions, offer views of the surrounding area.

OPPOSITE: Tower bedroom facing northwest
BELOW: Bedroom ceiling with carved corbels

ABOVE LEFT:
Turret with animal carvings

ABOVE RIGHT:
Detail of the zodiac frieze

OPPOSITE:
Ca' d'Zan tower from the west

FOLLOWING PAGES:
Belvedere

The belvedere is accessed via an external staircase, which curves around to the top of the landing. The terracotta balustrade is covered in designs of flora and fauna, reflecting Mable's love of nature.

The four sides of the belvedere are lined with columns supporting Gothic tracery, framing breathtaking views of Sarasota and the barrier islands. Above the tracery is a brilliantly colored frieze depicting signs of the zodiac.

Mable's birth sign, Pisces, faces east, where it can be seen from the front lawn. In the four corners of the tower are small turrets covered with whimsical carvings of squirrels, bats, owls, and cats, intended to amuse those privileged enough to see them.

GROUNDS
AND GARDENS

S. 56—Entrance to John Ringling Mansion, Sarasota, Fla.

The grounds of Ca' d'Zan are entered
through a gatehouse on Bay Shore Road,
one-third of a mile to the east. Designed by
Baum, the gatehouse originally doubled as an
apartment for the Ringlings' groundskeeper.
A long driveway stretches from the gatehouse
to the mansion, where it terminates in a large
circle. The driveway passes a small cottage,
tucked away in the trees, once occupied by the
Ringlings' yacht captain and his family. The
cottage was designed by New York architect
John H. Phillips, who would later design the
art museum.

In front of Ca' d'Zan is a lush green lawn,
divided by a walkway lined with Royal Palms.
At the start of the walkway are two lead garden
ornaments in the form of sphinxes, and in
the middle is a star-shaped mosaic, made of
terracotta tiles, depicting the signs of the zodiac.

RIGHT:
Swimming pool, 1920s

BELOW: Postcard of
the front lawn and
swimming pool, 1950s

OPPOSITE: Aerial view
of Ca' d'Zan from the
northeast

To the north of the walkway, near the mansion,
is a white marble swimming pool lined with
colored tiles. To the south, further from the house,
was originally a clay tennis court surrounded by
dense foliage as a barrier for sound.

To the east of Ca' d'Zan is a rose garden established by Mable, who was an avid gardener. The garden is laid out in a wagon-wheel design, with flowerbeds encircling a central gazebo. The garden features sculptures of courting couples, acquired in Europe, interspersed among columns, originally connected by a trellis. Completed in 1913, the garden is now the oldest surviving example of its type in Florida.

To the north of Ca' d'Zan is a smaller and less formal garden, also established by Mable. Consisting of flowerbeds and walkways with a large urn at the center, the garden was used as a source of flowers for arrangements to decorate the home. Behind the garden is a gravesite where John and Mable are now buried together with John's sister, Ida Ringling North.

THE RINGLINGS AND SARASOTA

The life of John Ringling epitomizes the American dream, in which a boy of humble origins becomes, through hard work and determination, one of the wealthiest men in the country. In 1925, when John's portrait graced the cover of *Time* magazine, his net worth was estimated at $200 million. While the basis of his fortune was the circus, it was supplemented by other investments, including oil, ranching, railroads, and real estate.

John's activities as a local landowner and developer transformed Sarasota from a quiet fishing village to a fashionable resort town. Ca' d'Zan played an important part in this process, for it served as a show home illustrating to other wealthy individuals what was possible if they too chose to invest in the area.

In 1916 John purchased the Cedar Point (now Golden Gate Point) peninsula and the old Sarasota Yacht and Automobile Club. Mable supervised the refurbishment of the club, which was converted into the Sunset Apartments, offering views of Sarasota Bay.

Sarasota Yacht and Automobile Club, Sarasota, Fla.

PREVIOUS PAGE: Aerial view of the art museum courtyard

OPPOSITE: John Ringling, c. 1927

ABOVE: Postcard of the Sarasota Yacht and Automobile Club, 1920s

RIGHT: John Ringling on the cover of *Time* magazine, 1925

FIFTEEN CENTS

TIME
The Weekly News-Magazine

VOL. V. No. 14

MR. JOHN RINGLING
Carnivora to the general —
(See Page 15)

APRIL 6, 1925

John's most ambitious project was a large upscale development known as the John Ringling Estates, which was to include a shopping district, city park, beachfront resort, luxury hotel, and golf course. The estates were to be located on the barrier islands of Sarasota. To connect the islands to the mainland, John paid nearly $1 million for the construction of a causeway, which he later donated to the city.

The first section of the causeway stretches west from Golden Gate Point to Bird Key, then a twelve-acre island with a magnificent home, dating from 1911. John proposed that Bird Key be established as a retreat for President Warren G. Harding, with the home serving as a winter White House. Unfortunately, the president died before John's vision for the property was realized.

TOP: Panorama of St. Armands Key by the Gibson Catlett Studio, 1925

RIGHT: Causeway to the barrier islands, 1920s

From Bird Key the causeway extends further west to St. Armands Key, where John planned a shopping district designed by landscape architect John J. Watson. Known today as St. Armands Circle, the shopping district is within easy walking distance of Lido Beach on the Gulf of Mexico. There John Ringling built a series of private bathhouses, similar to those of the exclusive beaches of South Hampton and Rye in New York.

On Longboat Key, located directly to the north, John offered land for a resort-style country club, complete with an 18-hole professional golf course. He also began construction of a Ritz-Carlton hotel, designed by the firm of Warren & Wetmore, the architects of Grand Central Station in New York City. Work on the hotel ceased when the Florida real estate market crashed in 1926.

In an effort to stimulate the local economy, John moved the winter quarters of the Ringling Bros. and Barnum & Bailey Circus to Sarasota the following year. Occupying 200 acres of former fairgrounds to the south of downtown, winter quarters was a training facility where circus performers prepared for the season ahead. It became a major tourist attraction, drawing hundreds of thousands of visitors a year.

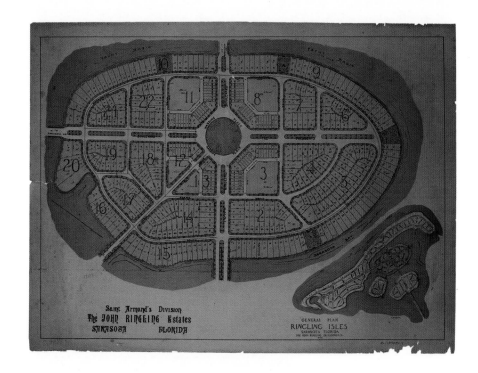

ABOVE: Plan of Ringling Isles by John Watson, 1924

LEFT: Ritz-Carlton hotel, 1920s. © Sarasota County Historical Resources

TOP: Sarasota tourism poster by the Strobridge Lithographing Company, 1924. Courtesy of Howard and Janice Tibbals

ABOVE: Winter quarters, c. 1950

OPPOSITE: Entrance to winter quarters, c. 1945

BELOW: John Ringling at an auction in London, 1928

RIGHT: Art museum, c. 1930

BOTTOM: Books from John Ringling's library

With the aim of establishing Sarasota as a cultural destination, John set out to build an art museum like those he had visited on his trips to Europe. Located on his own property, to the east of Ca' d'Zan, the museum was designed in the style of an Italian Renaissance villa by architect John H. Phillips, who had previously worked on the central block of the Metropolitan Museum of Art in New York City.

To fill the museum John Ringling formed an outstanding collection with the help of German art dealer Julius Böhler. The collection consisted primarily of European fine and decorative arts dating from the late Middle Ages to the nineteenth century. Many of the works were acquired at auctions in New York City and London. John reviewed the sale catalogues and educated himself about the works by reading books on art that he kept at Ca' d'Zan. These books later formed the basis of The Ringling Art Library, now one of the largest resources of its type in the southeastern United States.

The John and Mable Ringling Museum of Art opened for a single day in 1930, at which time it received more than 10,000 visitors. Following a period of closure, in anticipation of the publication of a catalogue, the museum reopened temporarily in 1931 and permanently in 1932.

A PALACE OF ART IN A SMALL TOWN IN FLORIDA:
JOHN RINGLING'S ART MUSEUM AT SARASOTA,
Which He Has Built to House the Art Objects He Has Been Collecting for Thirty Years. The Building, Designed by J. H. Phillips, New York Architect, Is to Be Opened to the Public Next Winter.
(All Photographs Times Wide World Photos.)

THE PATRON OF THE ARTS: JOHN RINGLING,
the Circus Owner, in the Courtyard of His Palace in Florida.

A VISTA IN THE RINGLING MUSEUM: ONE OF THE
ITALIAN GALLERIES IN THE NORTH WING,
The Doorway Comes From the Villa Palmieri of Boccaccio's Decameron.

ANTIQUE DOORWAYS WHICH COMPLETE A VISTA: A VIEW ACROSS THE GALLERIES of One of the Wings of the Museum.

THE LOGGIA OF THE RINGLING MUSEUM, FROM THE ENTRANCE VESTIBULE,
Showing the Eleventh Century Marble Columns at the Right, and in the Background a Marble Inlay Doorway From Florence.

A COLLECTION OF ITALIAN PRIMITIVES
in One of the Galleries, With Altarpieces and Florentine Furniture.

LEFT: *New York Times* article on the art museum, 1930

ABOVE: *Rest on the Flight into Egypt* by Paolo Veronese, c. 1572

Air-Plane View of THE JOHN AND MABLE RINGLING MUSEUM OF ART, Sarasota. Fla. J.H.Phillips Architect NY
SHOWING DORMITORY AND SCHOOL ADDITION.

ABOVE: Aerial view of the art museum by John Phillips, 1928

BELOW: Art school brochure, early 1930s

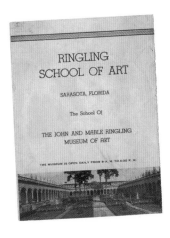

John's plan for the museum originally included an art school, where students would learn from works in the collection. While financial troubles during the Great Depression forced John to abandon this idea, he acquired instead the nearby Bay Haven Hotel and commissioned Phillips to reconfigure the interiors for educational use. After a brief affiliation with Southern College of Lakeland, the new school became an independent entity in 1933. It has since developed into Ringling College of Art and Design, one of the finest institutions of its type in the country.

Unfortunately, Mable never saw the completion of the museum or establishment of the school, for she died in 1929 from complications relating to diabetes and Addison's disease. Upon John's death seven years later, the museum and Ca' d'Zan were bequeathed to the state of Florida. The bequest was formerly accepted in 1946, at which time the mansion opened to the public, attracting more than 10,000 visitors on its first day. Since then it has welcomed millions more, drawn to Sarasota as a cultural destination, just as the Ringlings envisioned.

LEFT: Statue of *David* being installed, c. 1929

ABOVE: Chiurazzi Foundry catalogue, 1900

RIGHT: Statue of *David*

SCULPTURES

John acquired copies of Classical, Renaissance, and Baroque sculptures to decorate his many local real estate projects. The majority of these casts were purchased from the Chiurazzi Foundry in Naples, Italy. A number of the sculptures originally intended for the failed Ritz-Carlton hotel were later installed in the courtyard of the art museum. These sculptures figured in John's initial plan for the art school, where students would learn to draw from them, as had long been the practice in the art academies of Europe.

The most impressive of the casts is a full-sized bronze copy of Michelangelo's *David*, which overlooks the courtyard from the west. This iconic figure has become a symbol of Sarasota.

THE RESTORATION OF CA' D'ZAN

Since its completion in 1926, Ca' d'Zan has been exposed to extreme heat, strong wind, and driving rain, as well as the damaging effects of salt spray from Sarasota Bay. The elements have taken their toll on the house, necessitating regular maintenance.

At times throughout its history, Ca' d'Zan has required more extensive restorations. The most significant of these was carried out between 1996 and 2002 at a cost of $15 million. It involved the repair or replacement of structural elements and decorative features, carried out by specialists in a variety of fields. It also involved a significant upgrade to the mechanical systems, enabling better control of conditions within the home, which impact on both the care of its contents and comfort of its visitors.

Restoration work continues today in an effort to ensure that Ca' d'Zan is able to tell the remarkable story of John and Mable Ringling for years to come.

PREVIOUS PAGES:
Aerial view of the art museum

ABOVE: Stairs to the belvedere prior to restoration, 1990s

RIGHT: Stairs to the lower dock in disrepair, 1990s

OPPOSITE: *Pelican Press* article about the filming at Ca' d'Zan, 1996

Ringling's
Great Expectations

Ca' D' Zan dressed down for Hollywood to play the part of a moldering mansion for a movie version of Charles Dickens' "Great Expectations."

Terry Butler from the museum's greens department installed and maintains the greenery on the set. Three semi truck loads of greens were brought in from Miami, plus the greens department cleaned out vacant lots and any weeds on the Ringling grounds in Sarasota.

A wall was built around the front of the Ringling mansion to enclose the set.

The screening set is hung way up the grand gallery on a piece of set.

Rigging electricians (l. to r.) Bob Scott, Charles Hess, Josh Weinstein, Marty Petlock and Michael Verbil carry electrical cables to the set.

A cameraman waits for measurements before shooting footage of the gate.

A dilapidated piano, plus comer and stand in doorway are part of the props on the set.

Photos by Rebecca Wild Baxter

ON SCREEN

Ca' d'Zan has been featured in motion pictures and television programs, ranging from dramas to documentaries. Most notably, it served as the ruined mansion of the wealthy Miss Havisham (renamed Ms. Dinsmoor) in a film adaptation of Charles Dickens's classic novel, *Great Expectations*. Shot in 1996 and released two years later, the film drew attention to Ca' d'Zan and the fundraising effort then underway to pay for its much-needed restoration.